Earthrise

Earthrise

Poems by

Deborah Fleming

Cover design by Shay Culligan

ISBN: 978-1-952326-82-0

Kelsay Books
502 South 1040 East, A-119
American Fork, Utah, 84003

For Clarke

Other Titles by the Author

Poetry
Into a New Country
Morning, Winter Solstice

Poetry Chapbooks
Source of the River
Migrations

Fiction
Reunion
Without Leave

Nonfiction
*Resurrection of the Wild: Meditations on Ohio's Natural
    Landscape*

Scholarly Editions
Towers of Myth and Stone: Yeats's Influence on Robinson Jeffers
*"A man who does not exist": The Irish Peasant in the Work of
    W. B. Yeats and J. M. Synge*

Edited Collections
W. B. Yeats and Postcolonialism
Learning the Trade: W. B. Yeats and Contemporary Poetry

Acknowledgments

Journals

Blueline: "Ardagh Chalice"

Bryant Literary Review: "Peasant Woman in Gascony," "Perseids," "Red Fox on Zaleski Trail"

Cold Mountain Review: "Bravo," "Chorus"

Colere: "Isak Dinesen in Denmark," "Kumari"

Common Threads: "Mountain Song," "Pocket Watch"

Earth's Daughters: "Dawn, Summer," "Sea Turtle," "Supernova"

Eclipse: "Wind Horse," "Hollow Road"

Ecozona: "Venus and Jupiter," "Woman Sweeping at Boudhanath"

Ekphrasis: "Jupiter's Temple in a Landscape of Sicily" as "Jupiter's Monument in a Landscape of Sicily"

Evening Street Review: "Chemistry Poem," "Prophet"

Halcyone Review: "Back Stairs"

New Rivers Press: "Wind Horse"

Poetry Virginia: "Vernal Equinox"

Anthologies and Chapbooks

Open-Eyed, Full-Throated: "Heron," "Photograph," "Sea Otters," "Skellig Islands," "Song of the Goat," "Thoroughbred," "Wolfhound"

Source of the River (chapbook): "Isak Dinesen in Denmark," "Kumari"

Contents

Prologue

Greatest Man of the Millennium

Was it Gutenberg or Copernicus?

If Gutenberg, admit that we
For all our science cannot free
Ourselves from the firing neuron-
Mass inside the skull; invention
Trumps idea; fantasy
Is idle foam upon the sea;
The builder's greater than the architect.

If Copernicus, accept the fact
That we are merely accidents
In a massive universe
Greater than all human art,
Beams of pale light then dark,
Brief travelers on a speck of dust,
Players who never really learned the script.

Strophe I: Dithyramb
(Choral Hymn)

Venus and Jupiter

In evening's cobalt hue
The sun averts his glance
Behind the western hill; two
Planets begin their airy dance—
Venus, queen of morning
And of evening skies,
And Jupiter, her king,
Ten thousand times her size
And brighter, though appearing
Small and dim to earthbound eyes,
So far in circumnavigation
He sails around the sun.

Thirteen months apart
They will begin again,
At times so close the old star-
Gazers told the birth
Of beauty, love, or war
From god and woman
Trysting on the earth.

And cradling in her arms the new,
Here is the waning moon,
Watching for that true
Miracle, rebirth of the sun.

Perseids

Mid-August and the hemisphere
Now turns its head away from light;
Earth plunges through a waterfall
Of fiery rocks; white stars
Cascade into the endless pool of night.

Jupiter's Temple in a Landscape of Sicily

Ettore de Maria Bergler, I Ruderi del Tempio di Giove di Siracusa, 1891
(The Ruins of the Temple of Jupiter in Syracuse)

Palazzo dei Normanni, Palermo

In a circular hallway of the conqueror,
Landscape blossoms with shards of color,
Cerulean and azure sky-curtain roils
Above some island city's amber walls
Across a waveless, gray expanse of sea.
Meadow grasses veridian, verdigris,
Bloom with flowers, crimson, citrine, white.

At left, two marble columns rise upright,
Yet lacking cornices, crossbeam, or face—
Gateway now to nowhere or to open space.

At right, two peasant women in the foreground,
Their age uncertain, neither old nor young,
One looking downward, right arm bent
In attitude of expectation, patient,
Over her left shoulder, a basket woven
In the style of the place, crimson
Headscarf tied behind her neck,
Layers of her expansive skirt with flecks
Of citrine and of charcoal-gray descend
Below a blousy azure cummerbund,
Her bodice charcoal-gray like shadows on
The city walls. The other, her companion,
Bends, straight-backed, to harvest or to glean,
Her right arm reaching down among the stems,
Her dress and bodice white with coral lace,
Skirt falling into ivory waves. Both faces
Turn away, intent upon their task.

From everything the midday light reflects—
Walls, marble columns, flowers, sea,
Meadow grasses, jacaranda tree,
Skirts cascading in voluminous folds—
The standing woman's basket shimmering golden
So intensely that you feel the sun
Against her skin; their task, a timeless one;
The god of gods now vanished; in his absence,
Meadow flowers their vast inheritance.

Ardagh Chalice

8th Century, National Museum of Ireland, Dublin

Gazed upon by hordes, behind the glass
And shining in a beam of light, a chalice
Made of bronze and silver gleams with golden
Filigree and great rock-crystal; ten

Centuries it tarnished in the turf till thrown
Up by potato-digger's eager spade.
Among a hoard of jewels it was laid
In earth and covered by a slab of stone.

Gilt bronze and amber testify that someone forged
It with devoted hands; monks drank their sacred
Wine from it; they buried it and ran
From plunderers, intending to return.

The very air around it asks a question
Of our age: what object we now own
Will be turned up by plow or spade or thrown
On wind to puzzle diggers of another eon?

What will it hold, and where will it be stored—
Shut away where cherished things are hoarded,
Or shown in great display as something precious?
And will it be as beautiful as this?

Spring Cleaning

Under the cloth, a still life:
Heirloom table's grain of oaken brown
From an old house long since
Abandoned and pulled down.

Dust blown in through window-screen
And trekked through open door
Streaks pell-mell into the shrieking
Bagpipe of the vacuum cleaner,

Holding at bay the shifting earth
That gathers back its own contents,
Its wandering sons and daughters,
And all their shining monuments.

Bottle

John Fleming 1878-1950

On the lintel over the back door
of my farmhouse, once
someone else's homestead, a plain
tapered bottle stands beside
an old milk jug and butter churn.
A cardboard cap inside it
stops the mouth, imprinted with the name
of my great-grandfather and underneath,
"3% Butterfat or More, FOR BABIES
AND INVALIDS, Seal Kaps Pat.,
Nov. 2, 1920, Other Patents Pending."

I have never seen his image,
farmer/dairyman; stories of him
were never shared. He died
in my birth year away from home.
I want to ask of someone how he lost
the dairy, was it the crash? How long
had he been a farmer? Why did
he die so far from home?
But all who knew him
now are dead as well.
All that remains of him
are five descendants
removed four generations.

All that is left of unfulfilled
ambition is this glass bottle
that once held milk for babies.

Pocket Watch

Oral Windham, 1875-1920

In a cedar chest with his silk scarf
and tie clasp—the pocket watch,
its case engraved with sheaves of grain.

The veneer is silver plate, not sterling;
the works have stopped, long since
exhausted in wearing out the decades.

Perhaps his wife and daughters wanted
what he daily held in his rough farmer's palm,
wore every day with suit or overalls—

its nervous sweep of minute hand
and resolute stance of hour hand
counting off the immeasurable

promise of days and years to come.

Back Stairs

Eula Susanne Windham Fleming, 1903-1987

Beside the oak cabinet in the dining room
crowned with a china serving plate
no one remembered ever using,
there was a door that led up to the attic,
a staircase where ghosts appeared to her
and disappeared like webs among the boxes
packed with linens, china, toys.
There was a wall of pictures framed
the ghosts looked out from.
There was a curving stairway leading
to the landing; the ghosts
walked up and down. There was
a bedstead that bore witness to the births
of generations; the ghosts lie with her now.
There was a garden full of flowers—
roses, mums, marigolds—and pumpkins;
at last all died, even oaks that yearly
shed their leaves like rain.
The ghosts danced in them.

When the house was razed to build a road,
she moved away, but the ghosts hid
in cedar trunks, wardrobes, boxes,
and between pages of her books,
so that when she parted the yellowed leaves
the ghosts rose,
imploring with mute eyes.

At the bottom of the long hill the river
flows. Ghosts write their names
in lichen on a granite slab.

Ghosts

I lead my horse into the barn;
Inside he stops, raises his head;
The trumpets of his nostrils widen.

Before him, other horses lived here,
Long since sold or dead,
And grazed the sloping, tree-lined pasture.

Perhaps he knows of lives gone by;
He nickers softly, ears swept forward,
And lets out his breath in a long sigh.

Kumari

1. Kumari Bahal, Kathmandu

Behind the white stucco facade,
entrance guarded by lions made of stone,
you cross a cobbled courtyard,
pass high pottery jars that hold
wide-spreading ferns surrounded
by gates of iron. Brick walls
rise to a red-tiled roof.

Opposite, pillars support
a shadowed walkway,
pointed arches framing three
dark windows intricately carved,
fine latticework on windows
along the sides, branching
like a crown; lintels carved with
skulls laughing at life or death;
hewn lesser deities, peacocks, and doves
adorn the stately balconies above.
A notice reads: No Foreigners
Beyond This Point. No
Photographs.

Behind white curtains partly
drawn, the virgin Kanya Kumari,
also called Parvati, Shiva's *shakti,*
paces rooms of the sacred *bahal,*
not a vestal but a living spirit,
Durga—Ashta Matrika,
Mother-of-All—yet pure,
chosen from the Sakya clan—
those who work in gold and silver—
the Hindu Living Goddess,

worshiped also by the Buddhists,
for the flawlessness of eyes,
skin, arms, hands; even her stars
must with the king's be aligned.
Her feet may never touch the earth
because she is a thing apart,
and to look upon her often
is an act of sacrilege.

2. Kathmandu Valley (12th Century)

The Malla king, bored with wealth
inside a kingdom ringed with
shrouded Himalayan peaks,
played dice with goddess Teleju,
who came to him in human form
when she heard his sigh of boredom.
Soon he lusted after her,
but she refused his importunities,
and disappeared among the mountain mists,
whereupon he begged her to return,
prayed day and night, promised
he would lust no more. Teleju,
moved at last by pity of his prayer,
gave him the Kumari, said to him,
"In her I am found; worship her,
in a maiden recognize the goddess,
but keep her well away from prying
eyes, just out of reach, for men
cannot often look upon the god
or goddess, but now and then
reveal her flawless face, for even
faith must be replenished, the miracle

must at times be witnessed,
men must drink at the ever-flowing
fountain, lest they forget. Do not
allow her feet to touch the ground,
for though she lives, she must be found
pure and undefiled as well as beautiful."

3. Durbar Square, Kathmandu

Beyond the tables of bright-colored cloth
and vendors selling fruit and herbs,
wool, string, pottery, and beads, dark
Temple Teleju rises layer upon layer.
Black goats are tethered by the neck
to be given her as sacrifice,
garlanded in silk. Two stone
lions at the Dhoka Hanuman
are ridden by the Shiva, the other
by his *shakti*, Parvati, and by Krishna,
God of Love, incarnation in this world
of Vishnu, god of gods, preserver, creator,
and destroyer. Sun illuminates the streets,
but pilgrims walk inside abodes of gods
who must always hide themselves
and never gaze upon the sun.

4. Kyanjin Gompa

My family gave me up
to be the goddess at the age of five,
to personify both fruitfulness and purity
when I still played with dolls,

long before I understood
perfection of the living body,
to walk the palace rooms and let them
dress me in those golden robes
with pearl embroideries, my hair
enwound with silver cords,
my crown inlaid with emeralds.
All teaching was denied to me
while my brothers went to school,
as goddesses possess no need of learning.
I was taken out to festivals
when I rode upon an elephant
through the thronged and garlanded
streets of Kathmandu. When I reached
my gush of blood and pain that rips
the body through,
they gave me back to him,
my father whom I never really knew,
who then arranged a match,
and at the age of twelve
I was married to a farmer.
These from whom I had god-power
declared that now I was a common woman,
who steps bare-foot upon the dust,
cooks food, spins cloth, gathers firewood,
draws water, sweeps floors,
milks goats, bears children,
and worships now at Shiva's shrine.
This man my husband
slaughters a goat outside the door.
Then he orders me to bed,
and I, a goddess once, obey.
His mother laughs at me,
twice replaced by goddesses

of recent coin. Ten years now
I've been his wife, and I must find
my happiness in my lost beauty,
and on the lower hillside gaze
at the mountain rising in the mist,
the water plunging from the crags,
the towering snow-draped peaks,
the buffalo that slowly draws the plough,
the sheep that graze, the cries of children
playing as I never had a chance to do.
I dwell among the people
who chose me, worshiped me,
then cast me out to walk the roads.

At last I saw Parvati goddess
is all women; youth and beauty
are their emblem, for they all
have once been young, and all
for beauty strive. All mothers
once were virgins, and in their bearing
bring forth a new beginning
even as their menfolk
strive in loving to attain the goddess—
though they see her every dawn
through the haze of their own dream.

The miracle is this: In me the gods
have given back themselves as all
the gods are worshiped, brought low,
and exalted once again with every birth.
I work and know I was a goddess once,
who now must walk upon the earth.

Woman Sweeping at Boudhanath

Kathmandu

Tibetan woman bending from the waist,
dark eyes fixed upon her task,
sweeps with a hand-brush made of sticks
the cobbled walkway circling
the great white stupa,
her bronze face corrugated
with uncounted seasons of wind and sun,
dressed in her brown Tibetan robe and apron,
hair bound in a green scarf.

As monks chant and troop
in their saffron and purple robes,
past the prayer wheels turning,
under the line of fluttering flags,
below the Buddha's enormous eyes,
she sweeps the dust of the feet of pilgrims
with the slow patience of a god.

Peasant Woman in Gascony

1972

Under the shadow of the Pyrenees
In a field at the bottom of a hillside,
Before a line of locust and of poplar trees,
Around her waist a plain white apron tied,
In long black skirt and bonnet stands a woman,
Dressed as her mother dressed, and hers,
Below the stony ruins of a Roman
Aqueduct, spanning the valley and the river,
Legacy of builders long forgotten,
Raking grass for cattle fodder.

One-hundred-twenty centuries
Have celebrated this, her holy labor.
From her rose the walls of cities;
Armies ceased to march before her.
Farmers on her day paused in their toil
To contemplate recurring mysteries
Sprung from the generous, tended soil
From which unending harvest flows
And all the other gifts that she bestows.

Antistrophe I: Paean
(Song of Praise)

Sea Turtle

Queen of crystal water, she bears,
in the tides of her veins, the lands
migrating slowly across the flood
and sowing the currents with islands,
India ramming itself into Asia,
buckling into glacier-peaks, volcanoes
rising from the abyssal plain.

At the Japanese archipelago
she digs her nest and drops her brood
before she turns her face again
to her sun-washed peninsula
and leaves her young in the care
of the sand and the sea to begin
her long and ponderous journey home.

Heron

The sun has not yet climbed above
the hill that floats upon the pond's
gray mirror as the great blue
steps among the vines and briars
in the aspen-shaded shallows,
hieroglyph of the god of morning
with eyes that pierce the current,
shepherd's crook of his neck,
stilts like long reeds
that break the glittering surface.

Some movement in the thicket
and he sends out one cry
of *graak* across the water,
lifting himself into the air,
spreading his great wing-capes;
dragging his feet behind him,
the gray ghost sails above land,
ascending into ever-widening day.

Monarch

Transparent light of afternoon,
late summer chirr of cicadas
and the green frog's G-string note.

Ironweed blooms royal purple
like a glass of wine held up in air.

A monarch plucks sweetness
from the petals, carefully opening and closing
the stained glass of its wings.

Three Seasons

Gossamer wings with red and yellow eyes
on black zig-zag through sunlight,
propel themselves against the wind,
too delicate to outlast the frost.

Blown from depths of windy air,
whorls of feathers, ferns, and curls
shine purple, green, and orange,
too delicate to outlast the sun.

White petals blossoming on branches
shed raindrops blown by storm,
open to the early sun,
too delicate to outlast the wind.

Red Fox on Zaleski Trail

Vinton County, Ohio

On the trail through hillsides
twice shorn of woodlands
and regrown, I sat down on the earth
to listen to the wood thrush
at the solstice when the sun was high
and the shade deep, and saw
from the corner of my eye
an orange back slipping along
a pathway at a trot,
and thinking it a cat I called out "Here,"
and it turned and I gazed full in the face
at a red fox with expression so perplexed,
bewildered, as if I had been a talking stone.

It leaped into the underbrush,
I a scourge upon his sun-filled day,
he a precious ornament to mine,
appearing unbidden before my eyes
within a resurrected wood.

Dawn, Summer

We say "the crack of dawn," but it's
a seamless flowing from rich darkness
and jewel-like stars,

meditative hooting of solitary owl,
loud harmony of lark and robin,
golden line above hills
arcing in smoke-blue waves before
the great outflowing,

droplets at the tip of every
consecrated blade of grass
shimmering in fields of glittering fire.

Chemistry Poem

"Write a paper about your favorite element," the chemistry
professor said, and so the chemistry major chose carbon, and I
thought she should be more imaginative until she explained,
"Because it bonds with so many elements"; the physics major
chose cesium because he was the only one who knew what to do
with it; the astronomy major helium; the oceanography major
neptunium; the engineering major iron; the mathematics major
tungsten because it was so hard; the computer sciences major
silicon; the biology major nitrogen; the physiology major calcium;
the psychology major sodium; the political science major uranium;
the history major europium; the geography major americium; the
economics major nobelium; the business major silver; the
advertising major neon; the German major germanium; the French
major molybdenum because she was the only one who could
pronounce it; the classics major promethium; the philosophy major
lead because it was so heavy; the theater major mercury; the music
major platinum; and the art major gold;

but I chose oxygen because of the blood-red spheres they use
in those tinker-toy models of molecules,
and because—as climbers know at the airless roof of the world,
and divers know in the ocean's eyeless dark,
and the dying know as they cling to the last particles of their
        lives—

every breath we draw is our transfiguration,
every day a kind of exalted burning, like the stars.

Saving the Barn Swallow

Holding in her mouth the limp,
unmoving mass of feathers,
the little black cat offers me her prize.
I lay the pitchfork down and reach
to take it, iridescent blue, the soft breast
ginger brown with spot of white,
and I feel the bird shudder and know
it is alive, unfold its wings gently,
nothing broken, no bleeding
anywhere, and I cup it in my hands,
feel muscles struggle, stride to the
barnyard, raise my arms, and
propel it into air where it hangs
a moment, then spreads its wings

and flies, and I long to know the joy
of such release and the green,
wordless language of birds.

Mourning Dove

The mourning dove from the roof edge
Spied on our comings and goings in the garden,
Bathed in the sprinkler's gentle fountain,
Drank from its pools, regarded
Us with quizzical, half-turned head.

After a long vacation we returned
To find the lawn and roof abandoned.
She had flown to find another
Life in the wider world around her,
Like the bird whose brood has fledged.

Salt Lick in the Orchard

We used to keep a salt lick
In the orchard for the deer.
I believed they were magic
And at will could disappear.

Once I walked there in the dawn
When fog still clung to the air;
The folded grass contained their form
Where they'd slept the moment before.

Wolfhound

The wolfhound's back stretches
as legs measure off the furlongs.
Created for Roman warfare,
bred to hunt wolves in Irish forests,
now he chases rabbits
made of steel and pulled along a wire.

When he stands on strong hind legs,
his shoulders reach much higher
than a mastiff's. His coat is smoky
gray like Cliffs of Moher.

Head upon his paws, lying beside the fire,
he is an image loosened from his epoch.
The room unfolds around him
in a tapestry.

Thoroughbred

Raised for the oldest sport of man,
most finely bred of all his kind,
he writes a legend on the land.
His graceful neck descends to his long back
above the cave of lungs, coursing
river of his heart; long tapering legs
and rounded haunches pull the ground
behind him, every stride a wingless flight.
You think: speed, bone, blood. Even words
we use to talk of him take us back
a century or two, suggest a life of leisure—
furlong, downs, jockey, stakes, rail;
his names raise flesh and tingle
in the scalp—Nijinsky, Man O War, Citation,
Sea Bird, Hyperion, Nasrullah, Secretariat;
his places strut their pageantry—
Circus Maximus, Hippodrome,
Hialeah, Curragh of Kildare.

Canvases of history are painted
with his image: any rider seems
a conqueror on his back,
the servant a master,
so exquisite the legend
he creates of man.

Wind Horse

Do not bridle me today though the bright
morning beckons and trees shine gold in the sun.
So mild when you stroke me, I am not the same
when the west wind bends the high grasses
in waves like the sea. Flailing branches
signal to me that lions crouch. When ghosts
of dead horses wail to me from the hollows,
I stand on my hind legs and paw the air.
On days of wind I know my own strength,
my size greater than boulders, my power you
cannot harness with your bits and reins.

You have taught me submission with your straw-
filled stalls, barns bursting with hay, spring-fed
pastures that stretch as far as I can see but
end with a barbed-wire fence.

Take care. I can crush you with my bones.
Bridle me tomorrow when the wind has calmed,
when the storm has spun itself
into drops of dew.

Hollow Road

He paweth in the valley, and rejoiceth in his strength.—Job 39:21

Wind in high branches gestures to the hills.
Scimitar moon slices through clouds.

Beyond a bluff and broken fence,
lights come on in farmhouse windows,
little constellations.

Above them in a break of cloud,
stars rain down. My horse leans
on the bit, paws the ground,

steps off the road into the hollow,
stops, ears forward, raises his head;
his barrel tightens with a stifled sound.

The slopes before us rise,
waves that wash away stars.

Without a sign he plunges
into the valley.

Wild Ponies on Assateague Island

Recognize, in this small band
Of these once pastured on an island

And forgotten, desire for home.
They throve in marshland, left alone.

All around the wild blooms—
Murres, eagles, cormorants, loons—

But these were tame who now are feral
And gather at the water hole,

Their watchful eyes reminding us
Of what this land of ours was once.

Skellig Islands

County Kerry, Ireland

At the end of land the sheer rock spires
rise dripping from the water. In legend,
they were steps a giant sowed upon the sea,
a pathway to the under-wave;
they became a fortress for the learned
who fled the tramping towns
until marauders overran it;
then they housed a beacon
bringing ships to land.

Now, waves blossom into kittiwakes,
cormorants, and gulls, original inheritors
claiming their birthright back,
knowing that the sea will give them
all that they can ever need.

Strophe II: Tragos
(Misfortunes of Heroes)

River of Lost Souls

Gold King Mine, Silverton, Colorado, 2015

Once there were Midas-men who came to this place
To dig for gold. They dug out their treasure,
Then abandoned the mine on a hillside, laced
Water with sulfur and mercury, a measure

So deadly that all the fish in the river died.
Agencies warned of disaster, but owners feared
Loss of income from tourists, so workers tried
To stem the flow of poison, but, where

Water pooled stagnant with sulfide
And the mine leaked yellow effluent,
Instead they released the killing tide
Into the creek the miners called Cement,

And citrine and saffron water flowed
Into the Rio de las Animas Perdidas,
Turning the blue river of fish to gold.
Had they seen the end of what they gave us,

Bones of old miners dancing in their graves
Would still bequeath to us this gold of fools,
Crying "If we hadn't taken it someone else would have,"
Flowing miles down the River of Lost Souls.

Sea Otters

Where are the coats that greedy men
Sewed from otters' luxurious skins?
Hunted nearly to extinction,
They fed on spiny urchins
That consume the coral garden
Where iridescent sapphire fish
Weave among branches out and in.

Now, whenever they wish,
They float upon the calm sea-mirror,
And as we beg them back again,
They plunge and disappear.

Supernova

Hubble has witnessed a supernova
brighter than our own vast galaxy
with its gorgeous billions, watched
happening what already happened
millions of years ago, so long even light
requires to travel the distance to shine
in our minds, more radiant than
all that we love—the great Orion
striding in the valley and the giant
ladle turning on its handle in our near
universe, not one star touchable to us,
while we read our lost gods in the void—

and still we insist on believing ourselves
the center of all, doorway to paradise,
beacon of the mind outshining
any star, while the supernova burns on
outside our furious little history,
drowning all our squandered light.

Mountain Song

First there is a mountain, then there is no mountain.
—Donovan, "There Is a Mountain," adapted from Qingyuan Weixin

When is a mountain a mountain?
When Ordovician wind wears away
soil to limestone bedrock.

Mother of all mountains rises in waves
above the valley like a promise,
remembering bison and eagle, bear-stalker
and tree-hewer who strode toward the sun.

Lark and wood thrush among leaves
of oak and hickory call from the mist,
foxes and deer step delicately among ferns,
ironweed dances with monarch and eyed blue
to the song of katydid and cicada.

When is a river a river?
When sky-filled streams leap over boulders
to plunge to the deep heart of the forest.

Who has blown the mountain apart,
filled headwaters and dammed up the river?
Those who do not remember the owls
awakening to the storm of stars.

When is a mountain not a mountain?
When it has fallen into the valley.

When is a river not a river?
When it is filled with the mountain.

When will we know the mountain and river?
When they are gone.

Sacrifice Zone

Thou didst cleave the earth with rivers.—Habakkuk 3:9.

Where the great ice-river wandered
Southward to the plains and mountains,
Through the valleys rivers flowed,
Bursting forth in lakes and fountains.

Now the rocks are fractured wide
And the poison festers upward,
Seeping into slate-gray tides
That spread throughout the shattered bone yard.

This zone of sacrifice is bleeding.
Flares visible from outer space
Make planets ask what horror-dreams
Must shake us nightly that we never tire
Of plundering our only place,
Poisoning the lakes and streams,
Burning rocks, and stoking fires
On which our greedy hearts are feeding?

The waters of the earth that are its blessing
Are now transformed to iridescent mud,
The residue of our transgressing
What was once our body and our blood.

Bravo

Bravo: (Spanish) well done

Converted by the Spanish fathers
centuries before, the village fishermen
rowed homeward with their harvest, needing nothing
but the bright sea-girdle round the island.

The savage mind, the document proclaimed,
knows nothing of the future, lives for now,
will follow what we say like children,
so makes a reasonable subject for experiment.

In nineteen-fifty-four the blinding cloud rose skyward
into a shining terror carried by the firebird,
migrated southward on the shifting wind.
Villagers swept powdered ash from clothes and skin.

On Rongelap long grasses cover whitewashed
headstones carved with crosses in the yard
surrounding their small chapel with its pearl-colored walls.
Vines of the wild grape now veil the doors.

Marshall Islands: Ballistic Missile Site

Tragic men obeyed their great Director,
And so in nineteen-fifty-four,
As people watched in awe and terror,

Death blossomed in the island paradise
"Where hardly anybody lives";
The radiant flower billowed to the skies.

Then the Great Comedian came.
Men watched the earth explode in flame
And gave the site an actor's name.

Song of the Goat

Tragedy: (Greek) tragos (goat) + óidé (song)

You have called upon me in your time of need,
eaten my flesh, stolen my milk to feed your young
though my young starved, taken my skin to cover
your nakedness, stretched it over poles to shelter
your bare head, made my horn your emblem of plenty.
I was your shepherd and you named me Betrayer.

You placed upon me your grievous sins
and turned me into the desert to starve. I cleared
your pastures of weeds your cattle and horses
would not eat. You spilled my blood that your
firstborn might live, that your god might rise again
to ensure great harvest. You covered me with nerve

gas that destroyed my spine, watched while I died
in the fiery wind of your explosions.
When you see yourself in my eyes you call me clever,
remark my nature in yours: I am curious and sure-footed;
I learn quickly, resist fences, imitate my kind;
although I love the herd, I will leave it for better grazing.

I have asked nothing of you, but you take all from me.
My wild cousins scramble over mountain slopes
and gaze on clouds unfurling. I look past you
to a time when you have destroyed yourselves with greed
and you call upon me for help, and I on the high peaks
will not answer and will never again descend unto you.

Chorus

In all accounts, gods strove with gods
And rearranged each other's fate.

In all the higher tragedies,
The hero knows himself too late.

Antistrophe II: Eidon
(Understanding through Seeing)

Lenses

When I first put on glasses
I was spellbound by the world—
Shards of shimmering mirage
That formerly had flowed and whirled
Into a pastel camouflage
Now brightened into sharpness,
Precise outlines of things—strand
Of hair upon the floor, colored
Seashells strewn across the sand,
Tiny lines extending from
The ends of mouths and eyes,
Sheen of earth along a furrow,
Clouds building into radiant canyons,
Grit near pavement's edge, shadow
Marrying a fence post to the sun,
Red and white striped butterflies
Zig-zagging in the air, the ones
With round blue spots called eyes.

I learned to pay attention,
What it meant to visualize
The myriad images before me,
Saw how much I'd never see.

Photograph

For Edward Lense, 1945-2014

Wisps of cloud framed in the window
of an old brick factory, a relic.
Cumulus boiling upward from a wooded
hill, light reflected off the river
between branches of an old tree.
Even the pathway unfolds
like one of your poems,
leading to a new country where you
stride along the mountain ridge
above fields divided by stone fences,
northward the sea. On winter evenings
I still wear your old sweater,
read that poem of yours I found
in a journal, one you had forgotten,
discovered on a day of bright clouds.

The Artist's Garden at Argenteuil

Claude Monet, 1873

What strikes the viewer first are these small figures,
Woman's long white skirt and man in brown,
Holding hands and facing one another,
So far away their age remains uncertain,
Innocent or unassuming; behind them
Stands a wooden fence which nearly fades
Into the foliage beyond that shades
The white and azure flowers on the lawn.

On right, birch, beech, or poplar, the tallest tree
Reaches gently over them across the fence.
Inside it, smaller trees rise verdigris
Before the chalk-white walls of someone's house
Toward slate-blue shutters and the dark brown roof
Beneath the azure sky with clouds wind-chased
Across the chalcedony depths like surf
And driven into layers of ocean lace.

From overarching branches blue and jade
Voluminous dahlias cascade
Into the foreground, pink, orange, yellow,
White, but dominated by the crimson
Flowers that flow like waves and overwhelm
The man and woman; yet viewers know
This is mirage: the dahlias gather them instead
Into the garden's everlasting summer
Where blossoms of eternal union spread
In ever-greater richness year by year.

Vernal Equinox

I don't remember what we argued about;
it was one of those days in early spring
before trillium blooms, after the first
mating calls of cardinal and red-wing
when air is chill, and frost
outlines the leaves, but when clouds part,
the sun shines too brightly to see.

Your voice rings in the brook;
my heart, like sea glass polished
translucent and smooth by endless
friction of salt currents, is washed ashore.

You are more to me than you were;
more than when we were young,
surrounded by teeming springtime,
when all the uncertain seasons lay before us.

Bats

Among the rafters of the barn,
bats squeal and click
when I walk near,
warning in a language
I cannot understand,
draw close their velvet bodies,
webbed wings
I cannot touch.

Later, when the sun steps
downward from his beam
to paint the western sky
in red and purple,
and the barnyard fades
in shadow, they signal
in a speech
I cannot hear:
where the best food is,
how far, how much,
measuring out a world
I cannot see,

then launch themselves
into the evening air,
zig-zag like darkened butterflies,
tracing out across the sky
a code I cannot read.

Amish Doll

An Amish girl no more than three
clutches her rag doll, stares at me
as I wait outside the door
of her father's harness shop.
One sister, perhaps four,
pulls a wooden wagon
down a lane between
two barns, another runs
to catch her, blue skirt swaying
like a bell. An older brother
wearing overalls and straw hat
steps outside the shop,
turns his face away,
walks inside the cowshed.
This little girl stares on
in wonderment, her round,
pale face even rounder
with her bonnet tied
beneath the chin. Strands
of hair the color of corn
tassels stick out beneath
the cap. Her eyes are clear
sky-blue. Her green dress
reaches to her ankles. It is
September and a light rain
falls, but she is barefoot
like her sisters and her brother.
Her rag doll wears a long green
dress and bonnet, but its face
is blank: no ears, mouth,
nose, eyes. She is a girl child
and will have a child,
but this image of her future
cannot be made precise,

for graven images replace
the world; if we grow to love them
then we lose our love of
what is real. The girl however
stares into my face
as if she found some answer
there, though I know nothing
she has seen can tell her
anything about this stranger.
Though I have taken care
to wear a dark blue skirt
that reaches to my ankles
and tie a scarf around my hair,
I do not fit the image
of what this child understands.
I would like to paint her
in this attitude, but know
no portrait is allowed;
no art, no verisimilitude.

When I am finished in
the shop and step outside
again into the light, I see
her watching still,
as if when I was not
before her I was there,
as if she stared at something
she remembered, oblivious
to rain and rising cold.
She does not understand
the strangers' coming and our leaving,
things we cannot see or hear,
though we have eyes and ears.

Interpreter

In the front of the lecture hall
the interpreter holds the woman's hands
in his; as the speaker begins,
the interpreter's fingers, arms,
forehead, shoulders translate those
layered meanings into gestures,
the way inflections add or subtract,
the roundness of his movements
conveying tone without pitch,
syllables without sound, meter
without rhythm, song without notes—
every comment, every phrase
become a drama, dance, or tapestry—
arms and hands weaving lines in silence,
threading images out of darkness,
dancing away the airy abstractness
of words.

Car Trip

As a child I watched from the car window
The moon riding clouds, revealing its face,
Gliding into and out of shadow
Somehow fixed and yet flying at the same pace,
As I sped forward to land in a new place.

By day, fence posts and wooden poles flew
Past in a blur while behind me objects arranged
Themselves into silos, barns, hills, changed
Into a solid landscape, so I always knew
Where I had been, but never could I know
The land I still was traveling through.

Prophet

It wasn't the money I needed./ But I took it.—James Wright, "Hook"

In a BART station in San Francisco the ticket machine would not take my twenty, no one was around to ask for help, and darkness was descending. Suddenly a young black man hovered at my elbow. "Change machine's at the other end of the track," he said. "This one don't take nothing biggern a ten. I need fifty cent to get to a homeless shelter." His tee shirt was torn across his chest. I followed his dreadlocks and lilting step down the platform. "Put your twenty in there, and it'll spit out four five-dollar bill. I need five dollar to get to a homeless shelter." I did as he told, a slot just big enough swallowed my twenty, and four five-dollar bills descended into my grasp. I handed a five into his extended palm, whereupon he turned and disappeared into shadow.

At once the station master loomed before me, fortyish, white, clean, saying, "It doesn't help us when you do things like that." The young man may have used the money to lose himself in the fog of drugs, for all I know. What I do know is that he gave me direction before the train burst out of the tunnel into the light to carry me to another world.

Isak Dinesen in Denmark

I had a farm in Africa.—Isak Dinesen, Out of Africa

Have I lived only once that I am so many?

My father stayed among the Cree in north
Wisconsin, on the frozen shores of lakes
that have no name in English; traveled
the rim of Asia and rode downriver in the Congo.
My brother followed in his footsteps,
writer and explorer, while I set sail for Africa
and carved a farm on hills above Nairobi
whose dusty streets became to me
the center of the earth.

I rode across the tawny lion-haunted
plains where elephants, those great gray boulders,
rolled, and crested cranes called out clear notes
like church bells ringing from the treetops;
flamingoes, proud waders of the Nile,
sisters to the lotus, floated, sunset-clouds
above the land, the curve of neck and bill
so self-possessed like gracious ladies
in their gaudy plumes while vast snow fields
of Kilimanjaro shimmered in the sun.

Somali told me stories of magic horses
living in the river-bottom that rose at full moon-time
from oozy currents to mate with mares
and breed the foals of greatest swiftness.

Now come back to this, my flat and frozen Denmark
hemmed in by sea and sky, in this great house
where ghosts still tread the hallways, I write their
stories through the clear resounding bell of allegory,
though Europe marched across its borders,

and my losses faded in the mud
and death of millions.

Must we be forever separate from what we love
to know we love it? Can we never look the present
in the face? Where now the call of crested crane,
those beautiful flamingoes dancing in the river shallows?
Why can we never finally return?

The Moreno Garden at Bordighera

Claude Monet, 1884

A shadowed pathway nearly grown in grass
Winds between the foreground cactuses
And palms, rounds a bend to disappear
Among the leaves while jade and charcoal spears
Of cactus dominate the left foreground
And palm trees in the center sway and bend,
Teal, cerulean, chartreuse, crimson, yellow,
Flickering in layered light and shadow.

At center on a hillside, village walls
Shine white and coral, straight rectangles
Topped with tiles sienna-colored; green shutters
Frame dark windows. Church-bell tower
Rises over all, its Moorish amber
Roof cork-screwing upward into azure
Sky where bundled clouds conceal the sun,
Swept by tropic breeze or strong Ligurian storm.

Does the tower focus our attention,
Blazing in the Mediterranean sun,
Or does the palm tree, as it rises higher
From the garden's long and twisting fire?
Do the trees give way to shining radiance
Or swallow up the village in their burning dance?

Epode

Mendenhall Glacier

Juneau, Alaska, 2012

White water from the falls cascades into
The ruffled silver lake that spreads below
The great ice river called Aakwtaaksit
By generations of the native Tlingit,
Who say the glacier warns them in advance
And speaks to them of crevices and avalanche.

"Follow the line of bright green Sitka spruce,"
The guide instructs: "Where trees are dark there was
No ice but lighter where the glacier once
Plowed its way through valleys and the Tongass."
Two miles has the glacier withdrawn
In a single human lifespan.

The great white goddess wandered far,
Bequeathed to us the land and water,
Now pronounces thunder, now repeats
Her warning in her strophe of retreat.

One day, when all these tragic ones are gone,
No one but bear and eagle here to listen
To her oracle, she may announce again
The great antistrophe of her return.

Epode: Earthrise

In tideless darkness lit by glittering fires, our blue pearl wanders,
The only island we've been given.

Notes

Ardagh Chalice: The eighth-century, two-handled silver chalice was found by a farmer digging for potatoes in a field in County Limerick.

Peasant Woman in Gascony: Demeter, called Ceres or Magna Mater (Great Mother) by the Romans, was goddess of agriculture. During her festival celebrating the cycles of birth and death, called the Eleusinian Mysteries, all work ceased and war was outlawed.

River of Lost Souls: In June of 2015, Environmental Protection Agency workers, trying to stop sulfide leakage from the Gold King Mine in Silverton, Colorado, accidentally released toxic waste that flowed as far south as the Colorado River. The EPA application for Superfund status for the mine had been rejected by city officials because it might jeopardize business prospects, especially in tourism. Pyrite released in the process of mining was called "fool's gold."

Mountain Song: In West Virginia and eastern Kentucky, 500 peaks have been leveled, more than 1.2 million acres devastated, and 2,000 miles of headwaters buried by mountain-top mining. The oldest range on earth, the Appalachians contain the richest biodiversity in North America.

Sacrifice Zone: Lines 11 & 12 allude to Shakespeare's *Macbeth* 3.2.18-19; line16 alludes to W. B. Yeats, "Two Songs from a Play," II.15-16. Areas which are hydraulically fractured for oil and gas are among those places referred to as "sacrifice zones" by the United States Department of Energy.

Bravo: On March 1, 1954, the U.S. Department of Energy conducted the Bravo test, detonating a fifteen-megaton atomic bomb on Bikini Atoll in the Marshall Islands, knowing the winds had shifted and would carry radiation toward Rongelap and other islands one hundred miles to the south whose 20,000 inhabitants were described in government documents as "savages." Rockets carrying warheads were called "birds" by engineers.

Marshall Islands: The ballistic missile testing site on Kwajalein Atoll in the Marshall Islands was renamed in 1999 for President Ronald Reagan.

Song of the Goat: The Greek celebration of Dionysus often involved killing a goat and spilling its blood to ensure a harvest. Early Hebrew people ritualistically placed their sins upon a goat and abandoned it in the Gobi desert where it starved, giving rise to the term "scapegoat." The cornucopia, emblem of plenty, was originally made of goat horn. Goats trained to lead sheep into slaughterhouses were called Judas goats. In the 1950s, goats were used by the U.S. Department of Energy in experiments with nerve gas and atomic weapons.

Heron: The heron in Native American legend represented the spirits of wise men. In Greek myth he was a messenger for Athena, goddess of wisdom. In Egypt he was identified with the sun god Ra and cyclical renewal, his cry announcing the beginning of time.

The Artist's Garden at Argenteuil: Dahlias are sometimes called "the flower of everlasting union."

Isak Dinesen in Denmark: Isak Dinesen, pen name of Baroness Karen Blixen, was third in line for the Nobel Prize in 1961 and was a friend of Ernest Hemingway and Igor Stravinsky. Some of the imagery is taken from her memoir *Out of Africa.*

About the Author

Deborah Fleming's book *Resurrection of the Wild: Meditations on Ohio's Natural Landscape* (2019) won the 2020 PEN-America Diamonstein-Spielvogel Art of the Essay Award. She is the author of four previous collections of poems, two novels, and four volumes of scholarship on Yeats, Jeffers, and Synge. Recipient of a Vandewater Poetry Award, Asheville Award, and grants from the National Endowment for the Humanities and National Council of Learned Societies, she has had three poems nominated for the Pushcart Prize. Director of the Ashland Poetry Press, currently she lives on a farm in northeast Ohio with her husband, Clarke W. Owens, also a writer.

Kelsay Books

Made in the USA
Las Vegas, NV
19 January 2023

65915150R00057